Mothers & Daughters

La Palabra:
The Word is a Woman

*a collection of poetry, prose, &
photography*

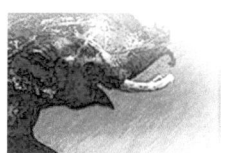

Mothers & Daughters

La Palabra:
The Word is a Woman

Editors:
Jessica Helen Lopez &
Katrina K Guarascio

Photography by Mariah Bottomly

Foreword

The relationships between mothers and daughters are complex, rich, unique unto itself, and ever changing. To say the least. Some are traditional and resemble a nuclear configuration; grandmother, mother, daughter, and then granddaughter. In either direction we grow. Our ancestors unravel a ribbon of lineage behind us and our future selves are ever born through forthcoming generations. Yet other relationships stem from extended kinfolk, tangled and intricate family trees and ties, and second (or third, fourth, and so on) marriages that result in stepmother and stepdaughter pairs. Some children have two moms and still others have none. There are those who regard the earth or the moon as their ultimate mother. As it should be.

Whatever the case may be, we decided that we wanted this anthology to be dedicated to the spirit of women and all the ways in which we create and sustain life. We too, then in turn, are daughters; caretakers of a cultural wisdom. As a collective, we set out several years ago with the mission to give life to creative spaces for the purpose of artistic written and spoken word. By providing workshops for women and gender-identified women, as well as various venues/outlets (live readings and publications) we honor the wealth of our voices. This is radical in a world that puts very little value in girls and women, and ultimately in mothers and daughters. Anthologies such as this one, writing collectives that decry the patriarch and call on celebration of women, local grassroots and global protests/rallies/marches that demand equality between all genders and an end to violence, misogyny and rape is vital and necessary work. This book is a crucial contribution and reminder to the world (our communities both small and vast) that women are life bearers, as well as the diverse daughters of what we know as Creation, and therefore should be revered versus desecrated.

Mothers & Daughters is the second book published as an anthology produced by La Palabra - The Word is a Woman. It is a collection of poetry and some non-fiction prose. Similar to our first self-titled book, it is an effort of workshop participants (in conjunction with the annual Women & Creativity month-long series), as well as a call for national submissions. In this collection you will surely find stories like your own, and some not at all. By way of black and white photography, you will be invited into the home and hearth of women, the familial ties that bind mothers to their daughters and vice versa. It is an intergenerational journey of unconditional love, compassion, faith and sometimes loss, heartbreak and even disappointment. Here are poems and stories of humor, exasperation, healing, and protectiveness. Here are stories about you and yours. La Palabra is a humble collective, a steady heartbeat, a clanging gong. Our publications are modest, but steeped with fierce pride and joy in the Word. An everlasting fidelity in the name of Woman.

Salud,
Jessica Helen Lopez
Mother, Daughter and Founder
La Palabra – The Word is a Woman

Contents

A Mother's Body

"Do not let this universe regret you."

- Marty McConnell

A mother's body is a tribute to this world.
Her body endures.
Her spirit battles—
Each night she runs a piping hot bath.
Bubbled hot with lavender salts to melt away the day's disorder.
Before the mirror she studies her naked body.
It's a typography littered imperfectly.
She makes a mental list.
Flabby this.
Flabby that.
She studies her body,
moves closer to the mirror
hunts like a battler for scars, gray hairs,
stretch marks,
cellulite,
age spots,
cancer.
Tears come
because she can't love this.

A mother's body is a tribute to this world.
She reminds herself. She scolds her negativity.
This body has given birth twice.
Two times her body held life.
She holds her fleshy breast in her aging hand.
A single drop of milk falls from nipple to belly
to the cold stone tile floor.
This is life.
This breast, fed her children.
This is beauty.

A mother's body is a tribute to this world.
Her shoulders are designed for her husband to kiss.
Melting silk white skin like a butterfly to sky
into wrinkled elbows,
into wrists and small hands.
This body birthed from her mother's womb
from grandmother's body,
from God.
Here's her troubled heart, her lonely prayers,
her worry and fears
wrapped in her empty lung,
her narrow waist,
her protruding belly that refuses flatness.
Why does this body cause her such sorrow?
She nourishes self with rich foods, salads and fruit.
Breads and meat—
It's too much sometimes. Cake and coffee adds layers of fat.
Yoga and running isn't enough to battle against this body.
She endures. She stuffs
those pretty summer dresses in the back of her closet
to wear again,
someday.

A mother's body is a tribute to this world,
a mantra to fill her unfilled belly button—
full of laughter and honey.
Her caesarean scars are a warrior's birthing-canal
into motherhood.   Down-to-earth
violin hips play a tune to soothe,
held firm with bone
undeniably full thighs
bursting from skin like an abyss—
sways with husband's dance,
rocks baby to and fro,
holds a graceful dress like an hourglass.

A mother's body is a tribute to this world.

Her strong knees, calves
and hallow ankle bone allow movement.
Her calloused feet sculpt purpose.
Her skin is tattooed in wounds, stretched strong
holding bone, blood, muscle.
Stormy eyes shaping her soul, full lips mouthing words of wisdom,
        maybe teenage daughter will listen.

A mother's body is imperfect.
Her life
interrupted
with insecurities   her weight   her husband   her job   her children
her art   her, she, I,
me
overweight with love,

here's   *my*
                body
                        naked.

Each night before my bath
I whisper,
I'm a tribute to this world.

        ~Gina Marselle

13

Cuatro Mujeres

My grandmother is fussing over
my mother's shoulder in the kitchen.
The air, thick with garlic, dense
in the perfume of troubled women.
There is a dance, a cradling of spoon;
this is how you slice the plantain,
peel the stubborn skins

away from the meaty flesh, repeat.
In the living room, my daughter
sits on the floor, legs sprawled, mouth
agape in red wild laughter, banging
wooden spoons across the tops
of empty pots, a few pieces of dry
cereal scattered. She gurgles,

sings to me, *Buenos Dias,*
a chorus of perfect teeth smile,
a parade. Abuela bursts, a chime
of aged rum and cackle, fingers
coated in olive oil, knuckles deep
in the proud work of a good meal.

This is how you taste for rhythm, let
the simmer of sofrito and adobo melt
between tongue and teeth. A little
more pique, a little aguacate. Hand me
the Tostonera, Sarah. We are – all
of us – this one sacred thing, wrapped

in the stretch of the longest
summer, humid air settling in the cracks
of linoleum, where the bones of us
hunger for nothing. Where we fill our whole
mouths with banana leaves, and sing,

and sing, and sing.

~ *Sarah Myles Spencer*

Nautilus

We are fighting with my father.
The house is cold and dark, the tension bathing us
in electricity like a live wire looking for a spark.

It dances around the room,
flirting with each of us,
Mom, Dad, and me,
but we will not be seduced.

The weather is miserable
and I want to rescue my mother from this storm,
so I suggest a walk on the beach because
I want to collect seashells.

I find many shells, cracked, broken, and weathered,
all of them reminding me of my mother
and myself.

Mom tears up and shares a memory
of her and my uncle as small children holding hands
while their parents lifted them above the waves
and I think of all the ways
I have lifted my mother.

A cold wave ushers in a nautilus, beautifully flawed,
weathered by its journey through the ocean
to land at my feet smooth and pretty,
with bands of soft pink hues.

I had that same warm, soft feeling the night
my little brother and I swam in the ocean,
Grandpop's powerful boat flashlight standing guard.

~ Brooke von Blomberg

Sunday Service

I have brushed my daughter's
hair forty three hundred times.
Till my hands were tired as old dogs
and her skin hot as asphalt
in an Arizona summer. I have lived
there, in the follicle, in the nape
of neck. The teeth of my comb, black
as bald tires gently scraping
while curls bounce like breasts
newly unbound.

I have brushed my daughter's
Hair till the marrow crows good
morning. Till my fingers uncurl
like the legs of wet insects.
Till I have reveled in the enormity
of this thing I have been given;
this holy wooden church,
this knowing.

~ Sarah Myles Spencer

The Daughter

The evening that I notice my girl is changing, sprouting
with hair into womanhood, I see crisp lines like
small black lightning erupt from the inverted
spoon of her left armpit.

The heat presses against the window, a boiling
summer monsoon and she is a sweat tangle
fast asleep on my side of the bed.

The butter pallor of the reading lamp permeates
every corner of my bedroom illuminating the
salt beads that congregate at her temples.

I sit awhile and watch her.

One arm is thrown above her head as if
she aims to catch a pop fly in her unconsciousness.
The other arm pressed to the small bell of her rib cage.
The arm is a branch a bird might perch upon.

The chest rises and falls like a doughy bread.

This is my life's purpose,
monitor the breath, the hair
that takes to her legs like
a brush fire across California
summer hills. To move the
lithe body from one bed to another.
To notice the faint shadow like a dusty
charcoal above the lip.

I know her body like I know my own.

I am prepared to be prepared for this shift,
this inevitable change of

the cosmological order of her being.
I am her ordained keeper of body.

And it is when I know,
that I must let go
that the real dying will begin.

That mother and daughter diploid cells
will have truly separated into their
own acts of insular creation.

That I must step away and watch
from the light house that all old
mothers retire.

Now, I hold the golden meiosis of her body close
this sweaty sleeping girl who almost
slips through my arms and walk from the buttery light
and into the greatness of the long dark hallway.

~ *Jessica Helen Lopez*

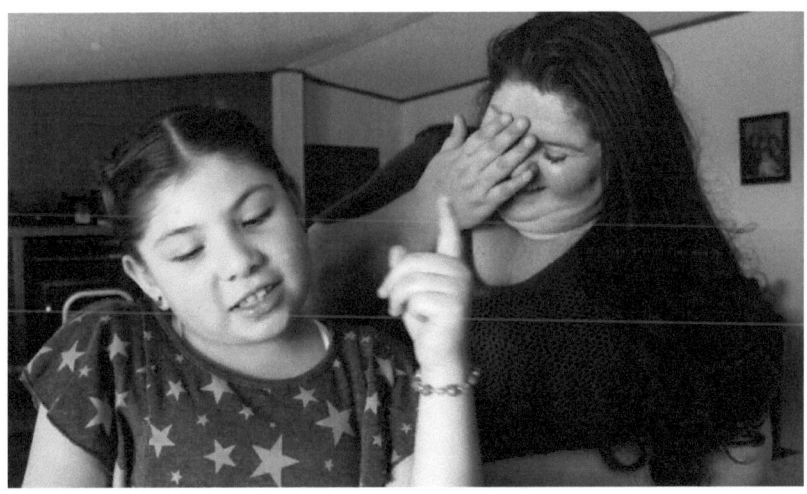

Solita

She is lovely!
With two braids that flow down her back
like the Rio Grande

Her face beams bright
like the sun
Solita!

This child made of tierra and duende
She was born the color of indigo
Her perception of the world is way beyond her years
and she will tell you so
She is fearless!

Never afraid of the monsters under her bed
She sings them redemption songs
to put them to sleep

She visits with the butterflies in the spring
and talks with them about their past lives
She doesn't blink at the sight of death
She stares it in the eye
and smiles at its beauty

She has the gift of magic
Putting people under her spell
Incantations fall from her lips
Disguised as poetry
She is my sol!

With arms stretched out
like rays of the sun
She burns away
My rainiest days
She helps grow my imagination and creativity

that stretch like sunflower petals
reaching to feel her warmth

~ *Nichole González*

Mother

My mom teaches me about life each and everyday
Only mothers can give you a rainbow on your cloudiest days
There is an unbreakable bond between me and my mom
How do mothers do it?
Every mom has a different story
Respect your mother before she is gone

~ *Sarita Sol González*

Eve

I am the daughter of the earth,
The lone apple that hangs from the old tree
In my grandmother's backyard
overlooked amidst the forget-me-nots.

I am dust and ashes in the wind,
Forever traveling towards somewhere
hidden away in a small creek or winding valley
as I join the sediments weathering a new path.

I am the rocks under the base of mountains,
holding strong to the heavy weight
I carry on hunched shoulders and tired arms
as I erode and decay under the pressure.

I am the carnal flesh and the carnal sin,
The leopard and the she-wolf,
embracing the power of emotion
as I entice men to their doom.

I am the naïve and the scholarly,
balancing ignorance and knowledge
on the blind scale of justice
as the world spins crooked on its axis.

I am the slave of mankind,
trapped in boiler rooms,
sweating blood without rights
as I learn my place in an unjust earth.

I am the seminal woman of the mud,
created by man's rib in an eve,

a terrifying guardian of my young,
as I climb the ropes to my destiny.

~ *Jocelyn Mosman*

Dear Mother,

Do you remember the time
they put the caution sign in our front yard?
A response to the speed bumps
installed on our road in early July.
Bright yellow, diamond warning:
Caution: Speed Humps Ahead.

We laid eyes on it,
exchange no words, yet
immediately decided
it had to go.

We didn't file a complaint to the city,
didn't make phone calls or ask any questions,
We didn't even bother waiting for dark,
but immediately sized wrench to nut
and unscrewed the metal tower.

I lowered the sign to the ground
as you removed the bolt,
it slid easily free.
Too easy.

It was large and heavy,
but I was strong then and I carried it alone,
placing it effortlessly into the bed of the truck.
Back when you had the Chevy, remember?

I returned to find you staring down at
grated metal sunk deep in the earth.
"What about this?" you said, kicking the stump.
"I suppose we could just cover it up."

I gripped the protrusion firmly
with bare hands and loosened it
right
left.

Like Excalibur for stone,
the metal post unsheathed from earth.
"That's my girl," you said and filled the
small square hole with rocks,
as though it had never been there.

We waited until dark to drop the sign off.
I directed you to a discreet dumpster
behind my old elementary school.
It was the same spot I would deposit
trash bags of beer cans
after high school parties
so you wouldn't find them when you came home.

You kept the motor running
as I jumped into the bed of the truck
and stealthy lowered large metal sign
into the near empty dumpster.

We toasted our accomplishment at the local pub,
fearless of repercussions.

Do you remember it mother?
Two women in our wild state,
defending our homestead
while the men slept,
no attempt at apology,
daring them with set jawbones
to strike again?

Mother,
we were feral then,
we broke up bar fights,
arm wrestled the boys,
and buried our own.

Stood our ground
joined our powers
enacted rebellion.
And now,
I hear your words spray
through my lips.

I have finally mastered your tone
for better or for worse.
I channel your strength through
my veins and I am proud, Mother,
proud and so very grateful.

~Katrina K Guarascio

Fierce Legacy

From my great-grandmother
I got my liberated woman stance
and my penchant for birthing girls.
She was fiercely beautiful
and beautifully fierce;

She had five daughters
and raised them to become
Young ladies; equally spirited.
A woman before her time,
she worked outside the home.

Until she was no longer allowed.
From Ohio to New Orleans
She returned to help her family thrive
She slowly sold off property parcels
to put her girls through college;

All but one, my grandmother,
who chose to marry young.
She left the family home a newlywed;
married the boy next door;
an Air Force man.
They were off to see the world;
Texas first.

Where their first child was born;
A boy, my dad, to my grandmother
At age 20, base and baby-bound,
she was fiercely proud;
Proudly fierce at five-foot-three.

They ended up in Chicago;
My grandfather enrolled
at UIC School of Design;

My grandmother worked
at an insurance agency.

She rose in ranks, despite no degree,
polished, successful, yet lady-like;
A Southern-gentlewoman to the core.
People sopped up her hospitality;
Cherished her open door.

She raised my dad, her son, to believe women
can be fiery, independent, beautiful and right;
He wasn't disappointed when
his first child came, a shotgun daughter,
Spit-fire, honey-haired, full of churl.

My mom, his wife, stoic,
German, mentally-ill;
Vacant medicated stare;
ragged nails; lopsided smile.
She loves me,
but always seems so distant;
My dad was empathetic,
nurturing and mothering.

He did not cave to society's expectation
for girls to be prim and sweet;
He took me camping; taught me to fight.
Instilled in me a love for NFL;
I grew up and married young.

Earned a college degree
in a field predominated by men;
Took on gritty jobs;
Park and Forest Service, even a Copper mine;
Went on to have three girls.

like my great-grandmother, I gave my all

to ensure opportunity for our daughters;
Like my grandmother, a hard-worker who
stands behind her man;
Fiercely loyal; Loyally fierce.

~ *Kerianne Gardner*

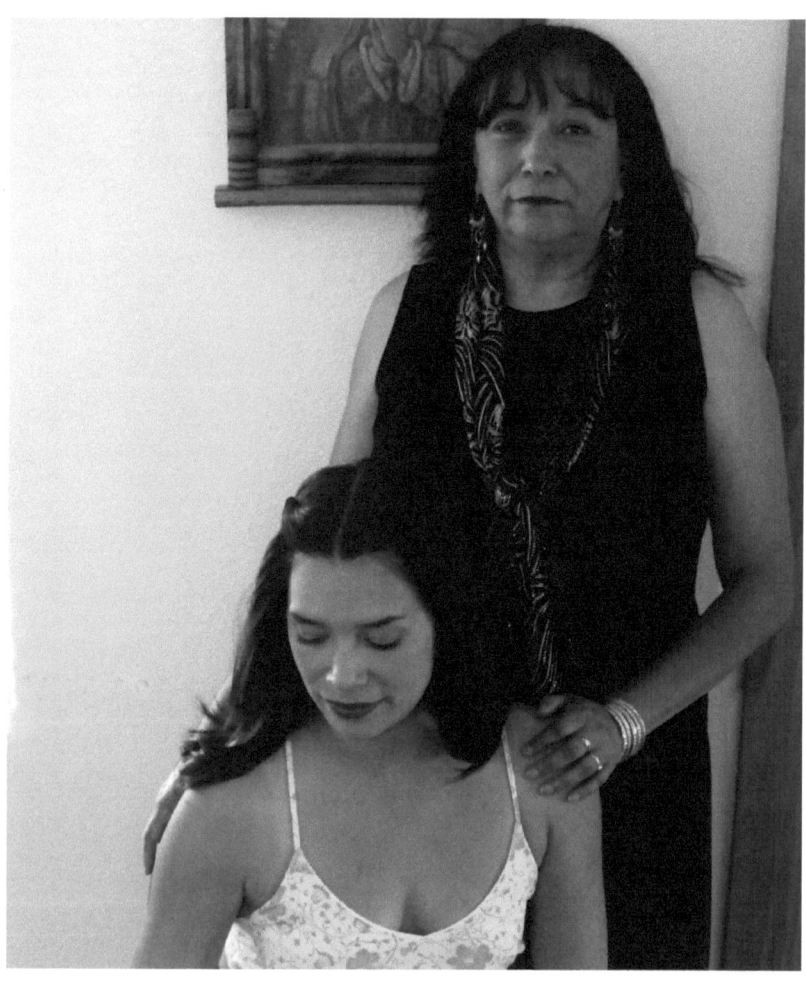

Dear Mama

Dear Mama
Help me swallow the truth
be more submissive, less opinionated
Teach me how to conform
Be less curvy
hide scars
Paint receptacle over my flesh
keep secrets
Cave in on myself when confronted
stop fighting

Help me hollow myself out
Tell lies
Let beasts feast on my flesh
admit it is all you knew to teach
and I will try those words on everyday
So you can be righteous
When you tell everyone I asked for it

I didn't ask to be
This portrait of hate crimes
Our family is a war torn country
plagued by civil unrest
ruled by rebel forces

We are chorus of tied tongues
A cathedral of brokenness and rebuilt walls
candle wax caresses
third degree burning into flesh
Mama, your citizens have all been exiled
your children have no place to call home

~ *Confidence*

La Trenza

"*Si alguien te pega ¿qué vas hacer?*" Ita asked. If someone hits you, what are you going to do?

"Hit them back," I said.

"*No empieces nada, pero no te dejes, ¿eh?*" Don't start anything, but don't take anything from anyone, okay?

"Ok, Ita." I nodded, looking up.

"*Y vale más que ganes, ¿eh? Porque si no, cuando llegues a la casa te voy a poner otra chinga.*" And you better win, because if you don't, when you get home I'm going to give you another ass kicking.

Earlier that day at school, Eric had pulled my braid. He'd pulled so hard the *bolita* at the top of my head snapped. I came home, my hair disheveled and loose, a deflated bag drooping to the base of my skull. In class I'd kept my face down, my braid pulled to the right side of my face so I wouldn't have to see Eric, wouldn't have to see anyone. Mrs. John, my teacher, asked me what had happened when I came in from recess. I told her my *bolita* had broken. I stared up into her crinkled blue eyes when she asked me again, but I told her the same thing, and this time I looked down.

Every morning, Ita brushed and braided my hair. My hair was long, and it fell past my waist, thick black wires pointing in every direction. She brushed my hair with a metal bristle brush, tiny metal soldiers standing at attention, ready for battle. She brushed and brushed until every tangle was out, pulled my wiry black hair into a tight ponytail, smooth and perfect at the crown of my head, then braided it into a thick three-strand rope. Sometimes my eyes watered from my hair being pulled, so tight I felt Chinese, my eyelids pulled at an angle from my temples; I braced against the pulls, holding my head stiff to make the process easier. I knew she wouldn't be happy when I got home with my hair free, unraveled, with only the last bit of it still braided.

There I was, braid repaired, in front of Ita on the couch, nodding, my eyes wide, while Estela Casas from the 6 o'clock news spoke loudly to the background. I stood to the side of Ita while she sat on the edge of the worn brown paisley couch. We'd moved the coffee table out of the way for more room. The gold cross she always wore lay shiny on her chest moving as it rose and fell with her breath. She wasn't saying anything, so I stared at her face, waiting. Ita stared back, her brown eyes unwavering, unsmiling, her arched brows squished to the center, so I tried to squish my eyebrows, and my lips, too.

Without saying anything she held her hands out, pink palms facing me, braced in front of her chest. I stood ready, left foot in front, right foot back like she'd told me.

"*No, mira, Prieta.*" No, look.

Ita stood and showed me how to place my feet, "*Porque así—*" Because like that—She reached over, shoved me, and I lost my balance.

"*Tienes que plantarte bien para que no te tumben.*" Plant your feet so they don't knock you over.

I put my feet back but this time bent my knees like hers. She tried to shove me again, but this time I stayed put.

"*¡Eso!*" She smiled and sat back down on the couch. Sitting down on the edge of the sofa, I was her height. I focused on her flowered tank top and blue polyester shorts.

"*A ver, las manos como le enseñé.*" Okay, your hands the way I showed you.

She made two fists, her fingers curled into her palm, her thumb wrapped around her bent fingers. The green center vein on her right hand bubbled when she clenched her fist into a tight knot. A nurse had popped her vein trying to put an IV in, and it had been that way ever since. I wanted to push on the bubble but instead imitated her and made my hands into fists, too.

"Amacice bien el puño para que no se quiebre la mano." Make your fist tight so you don't break your hand. She showed me with her hand, *"Mire."*

I nodded again and clenched my nails digging into my clammy palm, but I didn't want to break my hand so I squished it tighter. I looked at her face, soft, but young unlike the other grandmas at school who looked like *pasitas.* The skin around her eyes crinkled, accenting the frown in her eyes, as she showed me. She didn't have any eye make-up on; we were staying home today, and her skin glistened from the cream she'd used. She looked at my hands and nodded. I made the fist well, and I wondered if when I hit someone my nails would hurt my palm. I wanted to ask but didn't. She went back opening both hands on either side of her face.

"Ora si, pégale."

I stayed still, clenched my fists to either side of my chin the way she showed me, staring at her.

"¡Pégale! pégale!" She nodded, encouraging me to punch at her hands, but I just kept staring at her face. She waited again, but she kept nodding her head, as if saying, *Andalé! Andalé!* her eyebrows raised.

"Mira, Prieta así." Look, like this. She flattened my hands and put them to either side of me, and she punched, tapping at each hand. I blinked each time, worried she might hit my face on accident.

"*No cierres los ojos.*" Don't close your eyes. "*¿Quieres que te den un chingazo en la cara?*" Do you want someone to fuck your face up?

I shook my head, my braid swinging against my back. I didn't want any *chingazos* in my face. She went back to her position, her hands open on each side of her face. I was ready this time. I had to punch my grandma's hands, and not close my eyes, and keep my hands in good fists, and keep my knees bent so I wouldn't lose my balance. I stared at her hands and let my left hand pop out. The slap of my hand against hers was loud and my eyes opened wide. It hadn't hurt. And I hadn't missed. When she saw my face, she laughed making her whole body shake. My eyes opened even wider, my tight eyelids no longer possible, even though my hair had been rebraided. She slapped her thigh and laughed even harder, and I laughed too. We laughed till we couldn't laugh anymore, and when we were done, we both had tears in our eyes.

We wiped at them, tried to keep our faces straight, and went back to punching. This time I learned how to jab and cross, aiming my punches at different hands. *Right, right, left*, I thought, *left, left, right*. She showed me where to hit someone so it would hurt the most: *la nariz*. She showed me how to move out of the way if someone punched me back. As I saw her small fist coming at me, I closed my eyes again.

"No, no, Prieta. *¿Qué le dije de cerrar los ojos?*" What did I tell you about closing your eyes? She asked me, eyebrows squished in the middle again. "*¿Mire, quiere que le pase esto?*" Do you want this to happen to you?

She leaned forward to show me a small scar on her forehead. I'd noticed it before, but it was so faint I never thought much of it.

"How'd you get that, Ita?"

"*El cabron del Gil me dio un cabezazo. Estábamos averiguando y me abrió la frente.*" Gil had head-butted her when they were arguing and had busted open her forehead.

I looked at her face, and wondered why anyone, even her ex-husband Gil would want to open my Ita's forehead. He always gave me Chiclets and quarters for the candy machine whenever we saw him.

"*Gracias a Dios que se me borró con la Concha Nácar, ¿si no? Nunca cierres los ojos, Prieta, eh? Tienes que 'star lista, porque nunca sabes de dónde va venir un chingazo.*" Thank God for the cream Concha Nácar, helped it fade, if not? Be ready, because you never know where a punch might come from.

I looked at the scar, a thin white *V* that widened toward her reddish hairline, and nodded. I reached out to touch the scar but stopped, "*¿Lista?*" she said.

"But what happened, Ita? When he gave you the *cabezazo?*" I asked coiling my hands into fists.

"*Estaba lista, Prieta,*" she said as she put her hands up. We went back to fighting. We took turns, her punching my hands and me punching hers. I learned to lean into my punch and pivot on my feet to put more force behind it. I now knew to lean away in the opposite direction from the punch I'd just thrown and to bob back to avoid the other person's punch. She jabbed with her left and swayed to the right, I moved to the left and jabbed to the right, like dancing but with our fists. By the time we were done, my Ita's hands were red and my hands stung.

"*Entonces, si alguien te pega ¿qué vas hacer?*"

"Hit them," I punched out with my right hand and did a little jump I'd seen boxers do when we watched the fights at our favorite bar, The Tap, where we'd seen Mike Tyson my favorite, beat Ferguson there.

"*¿No busques pleito, pero no te dejes de nadie, eh, Prieta?*"
Don't look for a fight, but don't take anything from anyone.

"Okay, Ita." I nodded, staring past her face at the white scar near her hair line, her widow's peak, bleached against her light skin.

~ *Yasmin Ramirez*

To the Woman Who Has Become My Daughter's Stepmother

Your hatred for me is a biblical error,
a misstep or a twelve-year tragedy I should have seen coming.
You probably don't know this but when your man was my man

he spat on my face once.
I allowed the sinewy rope of saliva to stay there a bit,
sluice-loosed in the corner pocket of my eye,
the thin ridge of my nose. It glistened.

Opaque, a rivulet of starry-eyed diamonds
above the dovetail of my lip. A melting pearl.
My daughter has my lips. It was the end.
The grand finale that all historical tyrants yearn

for; the last act of warfare or genocide
or mass swan dive into a suicidal fuck-it-all-I've-lost
Hail Mary. You probably don't know this either but he ran.
He ran from my doorstep

shrill with fright like a boy who lit the wrong end
of a Black Cat firecracker. Odd how I
never thought to call on the cops.
Strange how our instincts can be pulverized to a dead end,

a pulp of echoless nerves.
Live wires hollowed and sleepy-eyed for so many years. But you,
with your terrible silences, your taciturn cheekbones
(high and pointed not unlike my own), so

colorless your glance, and a double-barrel shotgun
where your vocal cords would be. Buckshot
choked back and the smoke amasses in my belly,
coiled like a sleeping snake. Translucent, but

very much there. Very much real.
It is not enough to call you trigger. You hate me the way he
hated me and it makes me hate myself until I remember that I don't.

Hate me, that is.

That is an old bone I no longer worry.
To the woman who, after all these winding and unwinding
years, has become my daughter's stepmother.
Reminder, her body is not a target. Her spirit not

a pin-cushion for your sharpened daggers.
She is not your misplaced misanthropic antidote.
When you have imbibed all that is left to absorb
that thing that resembles compassion, remember.

When have you wrung the last dark waters from
the slack wash towel of his heart, remember.
My daughter is not you, is not your myopic version of me.
Is not him, a remote and angry island.

She is fidelity. She is deliberate song and stretch of bone.
She is the impetus of a holy and naïve love.
And lest you forget, remember. Her mother is a blade.
Your blood itching to be pulled to the surface.

>   *~Jessica Helen Lopez*

Lessons from my Kitchen Table

My mother refuses to answer me; stubbornly turns her back, continues flattening plantains with the Tostonera – has no problem feeding us with mouthfuls of our country, but will never admit to purposely robbing our tongues of its native language.

My father tries reason, *Don't you know, it is better for them to be bilingual?*

She says, *No. It is better for them to pass.*

I say, *Mother, you're a Puerto Rican from the Bronx, married to a Jew from Queens. My name so deeply rooted in history I can follow its tracks back to my Taino African Motherlands; taste the European slave owners drunk with conquering, taste the back of your hand on my bloodied lip – punishment for being smarter than your explanations, being unashamed to be who we are. I know why you did it. Why mothers stretch their own guilt with water, so their children can come clean. Have you looked at me lately? There is no passing here. I am goddamn beautiful, just as I am.*

~ Sarah Myles Spencer

Mīror

*"There are two ways of spreading one's light:
to be the candle or the mirror that reflects it."*

—*Edith Wharton (1862-1937)*

This journey is to open heart and fill the page with poetry. Fill the page to quiet the mind. The yogi's journey touches hands with that poet's heart. The goddess of woman ages into wrinkled toes and settled hands. The stillness of her hair whispers nothingness as she folds into sacred ampleness. Elongating spine into the empty page she begins with the omega. A fire of prayer burns inside to purge worry. Worry walks like a well-sharpened knife prepared to paper-thin cut a tomato. Slicing ever so gently as to not cut self to bleed crimson as pain flows like a pink jellyfish in the Atlantic. Motherhood is painfully tiresome. Oceans of waves guide this journey from tributes to disappointments. From a cocooned voice soothing baby's tear-soaked cheeks to tying shoes to tutus to honor roll to broken hearts. The earth bares scars from daughter's knee as she falls from bike's first ride. Tippy toes from her room to sneak into mother's bed like a ballerina en pointe on a sprung floor. Soft, smooth, perfect alignment. Her dreams are quieted my mother's breath. The night's journey is to bring comfort and heal the body from the day's battle. Evening prayers bless life. Bless the day. Ease worry with rested eyes. Rested body. Warrior hearts beat in time. From the womb daughter's stubbornness matches mother's patience. Together they hold each other up, as the day can sometimes be long. The battle is strong as teenager explores independence; mother's hand caresses her newborn for preparation for the day daughter grows into her own womanhood. One day ago this tiny-being perfect beyond breath gave life to her mother's heart. Mother gave daughter the only name suited for a miracle. Mir. *Miror. Mirari. Miratus sum. Miranda.*

~ *Gina Marselle*

Endure

> *"I have just been remembering how I used to make fun of my mother for 'giving up her dreams.' But now that she is gone, I understand that she had never really given up. She had simply shifted her priorities. She had become a mother, but she never stopped being an artist, a lover of life."*
>
> *–from Inventing Memory by Erica Jong*

My mother never gives up on her dreams. She shifts her priorities. She merely sets a goal and achieves it. Her artistic self inspires me to be something more in life. She isn't immortal, but immortality will pursue her in artistic form.

In this, I see now that giving up is not in her vocabulary. Not in our vocabulary. Giving up will suffocate me. Invent, pursue.

Inspiring artistic memorabilia.
Dance. Paint. Draw. Write. Sing. Reach. Learn. Endure.

Never give up on your dreams.

~ Miranda Marselle

China's Reign

There is liniment in licked fingers turning pages
of bed time stories
I know it heals

Rocks you slow like mothers arms
All of 3 foot 2 my savior
Smells like cherry Ring Pops and Now&Laters
I often come to her in pieces
She takes me as I am

Specializes in redeemed
Applies Elmer's glue and Crayola
When I come apart at the seams
Mama is her national anthem
Rolls off her lips like a prayer to ancients
Yiva imatanda zoyetu

I survive nights because
I can't imagine a day without you
Proof that God wears pig tails and
leaves jelly on counters
Maybe sometimes we all make messes
that are too big to clean up
Abandon them sticky sweet clinging

Trust someone more omnipotent will get it done
You've come in the form of a sun
I'm obsessed with your orbit
Pledge allegiance to the revolution behind your eyes
Little emperor your floor is the sky
I find comfort in your imperfections
Like war and famine
They remind me you're not to God to be true

There is liniment in licked fingers

turning pages of bedtime stories
I know it heals

   ~ Confidence

Truest Love

I have to tell you
I feel very fortunate to be from this place.
My dance class is held in the old school house
where my Mother first went
where she first learned to speak English
where she first learned to read and write.
I imagine her skipping down the halls
I imagine her confusion and fear
I always write her name on the chalkboard when I'm there
Fabiola.

~ Karen Vargas

Take Note

I picked up another piece of paper
You wrote on
Just a small note
To yourself
A list of things to pray for
Before you died.

A reminder to call in god
And angels
That you kept
At your bedside
For almost a year
That I keep in this box
With all the other things
You wrote on
Before you were gone:

Letters
Recipes
Grocery lists
Invoices
Address book
Bills

Your handwriting
Is the handwriting
Of the women
Of the children
Of that time

The uniform cursive
Above the chalkboard
That you were taught
To mimic, repeat
Nothing unique

Except to me

These are the things of yours
That mean the most to me

Your writing
The pen
Held close
To your skin
Your hand
Transcribes
Conduit
A connection
To it
Your incredible strength
Of heart and mind.

A lively discourse
A really good conversation
That I have
With you
And your pieces of paper
This morning
Like we used to
Over coffee, black
With toast and jam.

You're still here
After twelve dead years.

My hands
Exact replicas of yours
Small, thin-fingered
Wear the same ring
You wore
Made of gold

The same gold
That used to
Reside in your mouth
Until you got implants
And had your partial plate
Melted down
Into this ring
Onto your hand
Now on to mine.

With this ring…
Your mouth
On my hand
Your lips
Tell my fingers
Take notes
Your words
Leave a kiss
This pen
Holding my thoughts
Thoughts of you
Hold my hand
Guiding me
To write you
These daily sermons
Amen.

~ *Karen Vargas*

Descent

She leans forward in her chair by the window,
studies my face and asks, *Who are you?*
I remind her, again, I am my mother's daughter.
She just shakes her head, *But you are so old.*
I nod. Here in this tiny old house where she was born
I am forever 8 with crooked teeth and scabs.
She looks out the window at her neighborhood,
now just The Hood, watching what used to be
spin passed the place that has always been hers.
I watch it with her until she asks again.

~ *Cyn McCollum*

one-sided conversations with my mother

@ cemetery

ama, when you were alive, i never once spoke to you in english. now, ten years after your passing, i think there are things i would like to say that i've never learned how to say in spanish. for some conversations a dictionary is a doorway. for others it is an obstacle.
                                    it's raining today
like it was the day you died. the way it rained in the weeks after. someone said it meant the sky was mourning with us, but i've always loved the rain. and so did you. you rested when it rained. no fighting the sun's heat. i imagine you could feel the hot earth sighing and all the green leaves singing.

          your remains rest here. the earth is soft beneath my feet. the grass springs back when i have passed. i buried my braid here. with you. you lay here alone, for nine years minus one day, before they lay his remains beside you. the ground above him seems fractured, unsettled.

                              i am not the girl i was ten years ago, ama. what would you tell me now about death, about dying, about life.

@ kitchen

this is the kitchen where you made us meals without number. i watched you so many times. the sink is slightly rounded, here, where we both leaned against it to wash dishes. this is the counter, with its speckled yellow orange and green starburst pattern, where you made tortillas, where i laid out cookies, where we all always gathered.
                    it's been six years since moises stood where you stood in this kitchen. washed chopped scraped peeled seasoned stirred kneaded tasted where you washed chopped scraped peeled seasoned stirred kneaded tasted.

i wept. he woke the walls the house the windows the floors. the air itself vibrated and shimmered remembering you. this was my home again. where you had been. i wept amidst the scent of onions and tomatoes simmering.

i would like to tell you about his *atole de avena,* the *arroz con leche,* his *carne guisada* made without flour, the dish he invented with *nopalitos.* how his cooking often made me want to cry. though he hardly spent any time in the kitchen with you, somehow he learned, like you, to infuse his cooking with love.

i never learned that. something always burns when i try. maybe if you explained it, i would understand.   so much i would like to tell you about my brother, your youngest son, the last gift you gave me.

@ the garden

i remember you sneaking radishes as if they were a guilty pleasure. cucumbers by the double handful and fruit, always fruit. white grapes, red grapes, apples, oranges, bananas. a pan of sautéed spinach to ease your craving. *nopalitos* or green beans with a little onion and *chile. pan de elote* made without any flour.

you grew up close to the *monte,* eating the land's bounty. you grew up with a garden. i remember you poring over packs of seeds at the store. how you longed to grow your own corn and tomatoes and squash. you'd worked in fields all your life, harvesting the food of others. but i knew what you wanted. a little plot of land where you could watch your own food grow from seed to leaf-ling to fruit-bearing plant.

apa's hunger ruled the food we ate. he grew up on fried potatoes, refried beans, fried meat. he only allowed iceberg lettuce and tomatoes served at the table. i remember one summer we ate fried chicken until the thought of it made me want to vomit. i lived on biscuits and honey.

oh, the conversations we could have now about growing food and pesticides and nutrition and the benefits of fiber and fresh produce and hormone-free meat and avoiding preservatives and the causes of cancer.

oh, the causes of cancer.

@ hospice

i will always be grateful for this place. the kind and graceful nurses. the blue serenity room. the separate gathering area. the small moments of care. the visiting harpist. the extra blankets. the couch where i slept. the blooming plants outside the patio door. the vases of fresh flowers volunteers brought.

they never said you had too many visitors. and visitors came at all hours. a lovely place for them to make their goodbyes. no cold and alien hospital. the staff left us mostly alone that last morning. to hold your hand as your breath slowed and everything but your body fell away.

we spent very little time speaking in your last days. you spent a lot of time sleeping, especially after they started the morphine drip. and then you couldn't speak at all.

so strange, you lying in silence.

when i lived at home after college, you never called or shook me awake. you simply sat at the edge of my bed and started talking. eventually, i'd respond. wake up. and our conversations of the day would begin.

i think we both chose our friends for their ability to make interesting conversation. we delighted in talking to strangers. people always said we looked alike though our features were completely different. i remember we were both so charmed when someone said we had the same smile. do i resemble you more now that i am older.

@ road

in my first memories of you, you are driving. dawn. wind. the roar of the truck's engine. afternoon heat. gritty dirt everywhere. dusk. a thousand miles of highway unrolling before us.

in my last memories of you, i drove your body three hundred miles to its resting place. i didn't speak to you then. everything in me was silent and still.

so much we could say to each other now. things i didn't know then. grief. betrayal. pain. illness. i would like to ask you about despair and endurance. about the dimensions of the spirit. about your memories. i want to hear you again telling me every memory you shared and all the ones you didn't.

i'd have so much to tell you about the last ten years. people i've met. things I've done. who I am now.

i would like to share everything i've learned about the indigenous identity you were never ashamed of. i would read you poems, translating them all. i would insist until you sang with me. i would have so many questions.

you'd be seventy-one now if you'd lived. if you'd left apa all those years ago, we could have been a happy little household of three. just you, me, and moises. the three of us taking care of each other.

we could have been happy, even with the other siblings coming in and out of our lives. i don't know if you would have been able to resist taking apa in when he was sick, when he was dying.

i don't know.

your hair would be white now. it had so little grey in it when the chemo and the radiation took it all away. you would still have hardly any lines, and no one would believe you were over seventy.

you and moises would have a garden. we'd repaint all the rooms in the house. there would always be music. and laughing. we'd all take forever to get up from the table after breakfast, talking until our legs became restless. we'd take day trips and road trips whenever we wanted, and drive as slowly as we wanted. stopping whenever we wanted to rest or take a look around. no hurrying. no leaving it till next time.

@ waking

there is so much to say. so many stories to tell. your absence lives in me.

there is no way to end this conversation,
ama. it has no end. it will never end...

~ *ire'ne silva*

Prayer for Hummingbirds
on a Tight Rope Beneath
the Redwoods

To my daughter's hair,
I pray for you a garden
with six rows of tomatoes,
and twelve strawberry
plants that always bloom
the sweetest fruit, untouched
by insect and snail.

I pray for you a flock
of hummingbirds, wide
as the spit fire grin
of your grandfather, long
as his laugh out loud.

May you always do
your watering with dirty
hands and an untied
heart.

May you know the grace
of sun and rain; the feeling
of mud between toes
and fingers; to plant a living
thing with your own two hands
and watch it grow.

May you grow.

May you know what it is
to be tended to by the love
of a gardener.

May you know what it is
to be planted; sprout six rows
of wild summers and twelve
of the sweetest blush -
the flustering kind, the kind
that spreads and blooms
and brings the sweetest fruit,
untouched by insect
and prying fingers.

May you never know
the touch of prying fingers.

May you know yourself
a rooted thing; arms and legs
stretched into the earth; up
towards sky; mouth unfurling
a smile of grace and mercy.

May you be a tall thing;
a thing of seeing and knowing.

May you always know
the name of God
in all forms; sky and rain
and the kiss of a young
lovers perfect mouth.

May you drape yourself
unburdened, across
the horizon, braid your hips
a promise around the furthest
star.

May you dance; toes caked
with mud and fervor, beneath

every living thing you have
ever labored.

May you know yourself,
perfect,
As you are.

> ~ *Sarah Myles Spencer*

I Got a New Mattress

I've been sleeping
on my dead Mother's bed
for the last twelve years

She slept on it
another twelve years before that

Half my life ago
this bed slept us both
before I got a new mattress
two days ago

I threw the old one out
with the dip in it
that grew deeper
as the years passed
and really hurt my back

But I couldn't bring myself
to give her away
and tucked my body inside
the line and the shape
of the empty space
where she left her

where we left our
deep impression.

~ *Karen Vargas*

Mom

My mom
Writes poetry;
Loves to travel;
Strong German bones;
Can pack for ten days in a carry-on
Mesh bags for rolled shirts, socks, underwear
No frivolities;
Stoic suitcase
Sturdy black shoes

~ *Kerianne Gardner*

To my Mother, on the Tenth Anniversary
of her Passing

Dear Lillian,
Yesterday I packed a suitcase full of wildflowers and called it,
mother. I see the moon in every smile that could be yours. *Somewhere
over the rainbow* is not very far from where I am going, and I have
become quite efficient at attending everyone else's needs but my own;
ever busy raking yards full of other people's longing. Do you miss
me?

Lillian,
I dreamed a garnet sunrise in the shape of your bosom to carry me
home. I dreamed the rains couldn't wash away your storm. I dreamed
you loved me. An old blackbird nests on the sill of my collarbone. He
pecks and pecks and pecks; mouth full of me like bread crumbs.
Every spring I tell him to fly, but we have not yet been ready.

Dear Lillian,
There is a reflection of you in so many women I cling to. My grief,
dressed in trench coat. My fear, a gust
of icy wind. How cruel, can be the kindness I see without fail in
others. Do you miss me? You died on a Sunday. Your name was the
last word my father whispered through the scrap metal in his throat
before he left me too.

Dear Mother,
For so many years I have wanted to be a city of lights for you to look
to on the cloudiest day; a dream I have lived, a dream you could touch
with your hands if only you reached far enough. Did you find me
when I was hiding underneath the coffee table while everyone else
was laughing? Did you hear me crying out your name in the delivery
room as I labored? You did not hold my hand. Every day I have
shaped

myself into this woman. I have clamored for you, but you keep slipping through my fingers. I am so much of everything I cannot name. My heart, like David, packed tight with slingshots, my mouth, not always my own.

Dear mother,
There was never enough time. Some days I hate you for leaving me. I am a lost little girl in an unkempt room. I am unwashed hair and bitter sky. I am the yearning of your neck, wet with my tears. All I want to do is sing, be loved more than anything, the way only mothers can love, but you are never coming back, at least, not in a body I can hold onto and not let go. If I could, I would give every child a mother who loves them, an embrace to prove they are worthy, a bandage for every hurt. I would show you the scars, places I have road-mapped along my body, the mountain of coffee tables on my back, the garden of city lights I hide in my throat, waiting, ever waiting, for us to release them.

~ Sarah Myles Spencer

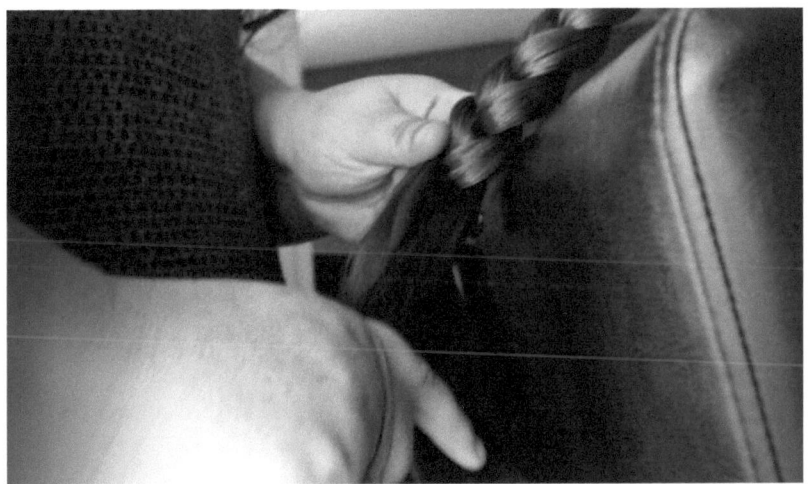

Plums

in memory of Maria de los Angeles

I

The tree was so plentiful every year.
A barrage of round ripened purple
overflowing thick branches and black leaves.
Fallen fruit littered the surrounding ground,
too heavy and grown to cling to limbs.

They were delicious.
Red center under smooth dark skin.
We gulped them down like air into formative lungs.
My brother and I.
We climbed those thick trunks
all the way to the top, despite her calls of concern.
She always worried too much.
Always wrapped us tight in undeserving wings.

II

This is to say,
you are not forgotten.

III

There is a childhood image I cherish
in the cobwebs of my mind when I think of her.
Shapeless in a house dress,
green with pink flowers, hair in curlers,
bare feet against yellow tile,
leaning over the kitchen sink,
so as not to spill the juices on herself.

Her hand, brittle as swallow's feet

as she removed the pit from her mouth,
still sucking on the tender flesh
savoring the simple sweet.

IV

She gave me more than the shade of my eyes,
she gave me the sight to recognize the virtue in the veiled,
to cherish the imperfections that make us so perfectly human.

V

The last time I made it to California
the tree was cut to its bones.
Only the thick desecrated branches remained
barren, fruitless.
It could been seen from the window
in the living room, where her faded orange chair held her.

Instead of working her hands over preserves
sweeping up pits and picking up rot,
she sits inside translucent skin
so thin I can watch her heart beat through blue veins.

They bring her plums in the spring,
some of them don't even have red in the middle.
Some of them are too hard for teeth.

VI

You smiled when you saw
I had eaten the plums that were in the icebox.
Shoving enough in my eight year old cheeks
to leave a trail of seeds from kitchen counter
to sliding glass door.

You rinsed off another and placed in my eager grasp,

never questioning my intention.
I remember the feel of your hands against mine.
Your touch like tender fruit,
so sweet
and so cold.

~Katrina K Guarascio

Also available from
Swimming with Elephants Publications

Some of it is Muscle
Zachary Kluckman

Cunt.Bomb.
Jessica Helen Lopez

September
Katrina K Guarascio & Gina Marselle

Catching Calliope
A Quarterly Poetry Anthology

Verbrennen
Matthew Brown

Loved Always Tomorrow
Emily Bjustrom

For more titles visit:
swimmingwithelephants.wordpress.com

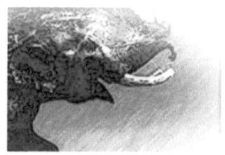